MANIFESTING

The Confidential Self-help Manual For Harnessing The
Power Of The Law Of Attraction To Manifest Wealth

*(Affirmations And Manifestations For Promoting Positive
Outcomes In Pursuit Of Your Aspirations)*

Lukasz Chadwick

TABLE OF CONTENT

Instruments That Are Available For Utilizing The Potential Of Your Thoughts 1

Does Scientific Evidence Substantiate The Efficacy Of Energy Treatment? 19

Achieving A Favorable Mental State 31

Honor Will Guide You To A Position Of Influence .. 38

Creating A Solid Oneness 57

Have A Clear Understanding Of Your Desires And Make A Conscious Request To The Universe 74

Losing Gracefully 86

Prosperity 94

Ways To Manifest Greatness 104

Subconscious Goal Programming 114

Step 4- Alleviate The Effects Of Stress On Your Nerves Through Maintaining A Healthy Diet, Getting Ample Rest, And Engaging In Regular Physical Activity. 123

Instruments That Are Available For Utilizing The Potential Of Your Thoughts

The process of materializing your goals utilizing the principles of the law of attraction is straightforward. However, the acceleration of the manifestation process can be achieved by utilizing specific resources. These tools serve a multitude of purposes, encompassing the clarification of goals, the cultivation of focus on desired outcomes, the reinforcement of faith in the manifestation process, and the enhancement of self-confidence and self-worth.

These tools have the potential to synchronize you with your inherent authenticity and instigate within you the impetus to undertake purposeful endeavors in order to attain all that you desire in life.

Write Down Your Goals

All individuals possess aspirations, yet not all possess the courage to document them. Recording your objectives can accelerate the process of materializing them as it brings clarity to your desires. By documenting your goals, you exert authority over the universe, compelling it to bestow upon you your desired outcomes. Additionally, it serves as a source of motivation to prompt you to initiate proactive measures, while also affording you the opportunity to commemorate your advancements.

To accomplish this, procure writing instruments such as a pen and paper, and proceed to transcribe your aspirations and foremost yearnings. Though it may appear straightforward, it is actually quite challenging. It is possible that you may have the desire to possess a sizable residence or a luxurious sports automobile. However, upon introspection, it will become apparent that your desires do not align with what you truly want.

Prior to documenting a goal or aspiration, carefully contemplate whether you genuinely desire its attainment by questioning yourself, "Is this truly what I desire?" at least five instances. However, what compels you to undertake this action? The reason behind this is that you solely realize the aspirations that genuinely align with your innermost desires.

As an illustration, suppose your parents hold the desire for you to pursue a legal profession, consequently leading to your decision to pen down the statement "I aspire to become a lawyer." However, within the depths of your innermost being, lies a profound longing to embrace a career in veterinary medicine. Pursuing a career in law is not aligned with your dharma, and it fails to elicit a sense of happiness within you. Therefore, it is probable that you will encounter considerable challenges throughout your experience within law school. Additionally, if you were to successfully pursue a career as a lawyer, it is plausible that your overall energy level would be diminished, impeding your ability to materialize your aspirations pertaining to establishing a fulfilling family life or engaging in extensive global travel.

Take note of the aspirations that genuinely evoke exhilaration and elation within your heart. When experiencing moments of despair, affix the paper to either the wall of your bedroom or the door of your refrigerator. By adopting this approach, you will have the opportunity to view it on a daily basis.

Adopt A Positive Mindset

As previously stated, the majority of individuals were led to believe that they are not deserving of their desires in life. Thus, we devote the majority of our lifetime believing that we are bereft of the eligibility to harbor ambitious aspirations.

In order to attain your objectives, it is imperative to embrace a constructive state of mind. It is imperative that you relinquish all detrimental beliefs that have persisted throughout your lifetime, and instead embrace the conviction that you are deserving of a fulfilling romantic partnership, a prosperous professional trajectory, and a sound financial existence. One must have unwavering faith in the possibility of transforming into the desired individual - whether it be a writer, lawyer, chef, artist, tech tycoon, or a recipient of the prestigious Grammy award.

To accomplish this, allocate sufficient time to attentively observe your thoughts and give heed to your internal dialogues. Do you engage in self-critical dialogue such as "you possess unattractive traits," "you have excessive weight," "you lack capability," "you demonstrate low intelligence," or "you are destined to never fulfill your aspirations"? If such thoughts have been occupying your mind, it is imperative that you put an end to them.

It is essential for you to become your own source of encouragement and support. It is imperative that you consistently affirm to yourself your ability to accomplish the task. It is crucial that you remind yourself daily that you are worthy of all the blessings the cosmos has in store for you.

Create A Visual Board

A visual board serves as an instrument for actualizing your aspirations by facilitating clarity in defining your dreams. It facilitates one's ability to focus on their objectives. If your aspiration is to lead a life of opulence, it is somewhat indeterminate. To provide further elucidation, please proceed to extract pictorial representations that symbolize the desired aspects of your ideal lifestyle. One may choose to remove images of designer handbags, high-end automobiles, grand residences with ten bedrooms, academic degrees, and picturesque destinations for holiday travels. Arrange all of those photographs onto a suitable surface such as a piece of plywood, cardboard, or a cork board.

Incorporate inspiring terms that epitomize the desired emotions for each day, such as "joyful," "excellent," "prosperous," "accomplished," "energetic," "adored," "resilient," "well," and "compassionate."

Ensure that you diligently observe your vision board on a daily basis. Please affix it to either your office wall or bedroom wall. Each morning, take a moment to observe your board. Please shut your eyes and envision yourself presently experiencing the realization of your aspirations. Experience the elation within your heart as you gaze upon the photographs. This amplifies your vibrational frequency and accelerates the process of manifestation.

Affirmations

Affirmations consist of positive language that is repetitively expressed for oneself. Uttering affirmations allows for the exploration of uncharted possibilities. It helps you think positively and shake off negative thoughts.

One should not underestimate the potential impact that words can wield. The power of words can exert a tremendous impact on one's fate. Therefore, it is crucial to be mindful of one's internal discourse and ensure that one consistently engages in positive and empowering self-talk.

Please adhere to these guidelines when creating your affirmations.

Ensure that your assertions encompass positivity. Kindly refrain from the use of negative language, including words such as 'can't,' 'don't,' and 'not'.

Develop affirmations that possess simplicity in pronunciation and are readily retained in memory.

Please compose your sentences using the present tense. In this manner, you will perceive the affirmation to be genuine. Rather than using the phrase "I will be rich," it is more appropriate to state "I am already affluent."

Recite positive affirmations that elicit a sense of well-being. Refrain from uttering affirmations that elicit negative emotions. For instance, should the act of proclaiming "I am affluent" evoke discomfort by seeming untruthful, one may opt to express "I am currently engaged in the pursuit of monetary prosperity" as an alternative.

This book contains affirmative statements that can be utilized to manifest love, wealth, happiness, and success. These affirmations are helpful. However, there is no obligation for you to express those thoughts if they do not elicit a sense of comfort or satisfaction within you. One may constantly generate affirmations that are effective for oneself.

Keep A Gratitude Journal

Expressing gratitude can evoke positive emotions within you and elevate your vibrational frequency. When one expresses gratitude for the things they possess, they are actively drawing positive experiences and circumstances into their existence.

Nevertheless, expressing gratitude not only expedites the process of materializing desired outcomes but also enhances physical well-being and reduces the burden of stress. Furthermore, it enhances your sociability. It facilitates the establishment and cultivation of more profound interpersonal connections. Furthermore, it enhances one's character and demeanor. It cultivates a mindset of reduced materialism and self-centeredness. It cultivates a deeper sense of spirituality within oneself. It prompts individuals to acknowledge their blessings, consequently enhancing their self-esteem.

In order to fully access the advantages of gratitude, it is advisable to record daily instances of gratitude in a dedicated journal. This journal does not necessitate sophistication; a plain notebook can suffice. However, should you desire to enhance the uniqueness of this journal, it is possible to acquire a higher-priced alternative.

Upon awakening each day, retrieve your journal and record expressions of gratitude and blessings. Compile a comprehensive list delineating all the aspects for which you experience gratitude, including but not limited to:

- Your parents. While they might occasionally cause frustration, they bestowed upon you the gift of existence and selflessly made sacrifices to ensure

you were afforded a prosperous existence.
- Your siblings. Despite being considered your adversaries, they will remain steadfast in their support of you, regardless of the circumstances.
- Your job. Although you may experience occasional circumstances where your job is burdensome, it provides you with the means to sustain your basic needs such as nourishment and shelter.

Your residence and vehicle. If you possess these, your fortune exceeds that of the majority of individuals worldwide.
- Your bank balance. When one expresses gratitude for the current wealth they possess, they are effectively summoning additional financial abundance into their existence.
- Your life. There is a substantial number of individuals who are experiencing the harrowing effects of cancer and various other diseases that pose a grave risk to their lives. Therefore, if one is in a state of being

alive and possessing good health, they can be considered fortunate.

Please ensure a minimum of ten items are written each day. Subsequently, allocate a sufficient amount of time to thoroughly peruse all that you have penned. This exercise elevates your vibrational frequency and establishes harmony with your aspirations.

Create a Catalog of Favorable Aspects

This particular instrument bears some resemblance to a gratitude inventory. Each evening, prior to retiring for the night, it is beneficial to record all the favorable occurrences experienced throughout the course of the day. Here's a sample list:

"I am experiencing a great sense of joyfulness this day due to the following reasons:

I was granted complimentary call minutes from my service provider.

I consumed a serving of chocolate ice cream.

I departed the office punctually.

My employer expressed their satisfaction with my performance.
I had the pleasure of viewing an exceptional film.

I received a telephone call from my closest companion.
This remarkable physical activity elevates your vibrational frequency and harmonizes your aspirations.
List of Anticipated Events and Experiences
By directing your attention towards anticipated events or achievements, you experience a heightened sense of enthusiasm and contentment. To evoke such an emotion, I invite you to record the anticipated events and aspirations you have for the forthcoming year. Subsequently, make it a habit to peruse the aforementioned list on a daily basis. This activity instills positive emotions, enhancing your ability to manifest your deepest aspirations.
Think Happy Thoughts
Whenever you find yourself engaging in negative thinking, promptly substitute

those thoughts with positive ones. For instance, if you find yourself engrossed in contemplation of your former partner and the anguish they caused, promptly substitute this mental preoccupation with a fond reminiscence from a beloved film of romantic nature. This would immediately elevate your energetic frequency.

When experiencing melancholy, I present to you an inventory of 50 optimistic ideas that might provide solace:

The endearing nature of your companion animal.

The olfactory experience of the seashore

The large waves offer ample surfing opportunities throughout the day.

Engaging in intimate embrace with your significant other.

Eating your favorite food

Your dream house

Your dream job

The projects that evoke your passion.

Puppies

Subjects of your deep interest

The aroma emanating from freshly printed literature.
The aroma of newly-blossomed flowers or brewed coffee.
A visually captivating sunrise or sunset
What actions you would undertake on the day you receive your salary
Mornings with your lover
A laughing baby
A funny movie scene
Your supportive parents
An individual who possesses unwavering love and acceptance for you, regardless of circumstances or conditions.
Sunsets and sunrises
Fancy tea cups
A beautiful painting
The perfect black dress
Shopping
A favorable musical composition that you encountered via the radio.
Cherries
Beautiful birds
Delicious birthday cake
Singing in the rain
The tactile quality of a cashmere jumper

Peace
Fried shrimp
Watching the stars
Good hair day
Having a long bath
Your family
Your celebrity crush
The sky
The view of the Eiffel Tower
A commendation that was bestowed upon you earlier today.
Delicious biscuits
A cute cat
The auditory presence of children engaged in recreational activities.
Motivating tales of ascending from poverty to prosperity.
Holiday parades
Thanksgiving turkey
The winning touchdown
Sexy Australian accents
A serving of high-quality, pricy wine.
Apple pie
According to Peter Pan, "Cultivate positive thoughts, and you shall experience the exhilaration of flight." Positive thinking not only enables

personal growth but also attracts one's deepest desires and aspirations.

Avoid Self-Serving Thoughts

In order to actualize one's desires in life, it is imperative to refrain from indulging in envy, which poses as a significant hazard. Jealousy ruins interpersonal connections and contributes to heightened levels of stress. Furthermore, it incites individuals to commit actions that undermine the well-being and standing of others. Envy deprives one of joy and impedes the acquisition of desired achievements in life.

It is imperative that you prioritize the cultivation of elevated thoughts and extend well-wishes of happiness and success to others. You must refrain from indulging in arrogant, disparaging, critical, belittling, and discerning thoughts. Keep your thoughts pure.

Think of Funny Thoughts

Humor is powerful. It enhances the secretion of serotonin, resulting in stress reduction. Indeed, films and humorous anecdotes are equally efficacious in alleviating symptoms of depression. To maintain an elevated vibrational frequency, particularly amidst challenging circumstances, engage in the practice of sharing humorous anecdotes with companions or indulging in the viewing of an enjoyable cinematic production.

These tools are simple to utilize. There is no necessity to employ complex scientific principles to attract the desired trajectory of one's life. You simply need to enrich your thoughts with uplifting and motivational ideas.

Does Scientific Evidence Substantiate The Efficacy Of Energy Treatment?

Although the scientific assessment of certain aspects of energy therapy, such as the concept of body energy, presents challenges, there is considerable evidence substantiating the efficacy of these therapeutic approaches in addressing specific medical conditions.

Based on the conclusions drawn from a scientific study, it has been determined that a solitary session of energy medicine treatment holds the potential to alleviate symptoms associated with carpal tunnel syndrome and improve emotional well-being. It is plausible that its influence extends positively to stress reduction, enhanced well-being, and improved sleep quality. The professionals conducted the half-hour sessions in close proximity, employing delicate and stationary physical contact in certain cases.

Additionally, research studies investigating the efficacy of acupressure, Reiki, and acupuncture are also provided below:

- Acupressure studies

The results obtained from conducting an experiment provide compelling evidence that acupressure has the potential to alleviate both the discomfort associated with labor and the duration of contractions. Further high-quality experiments, nonetheless, are necessary to corroborate these findings.

The study's findings stipulated that acupressure is a viable, secure, and affordable alternative to surgical interventions for individuals suffering from chronic lower back pain.

- Reiki investigation

A concise study published in the year 2021 assessed the effectiveness of Reiki, physiotherapy, and pharmacological intervention in alleviating low back pain and improving functional abilities in individuals diagnosed with intervertebral disk herniation. Based on the conclusions drawn, Reiki proves to be a cost-effective modality for prompt pain reduction and improved performance in daily tasks.

Acupuncture has proven efficacy in alleviating symptoms associated with migraine and fibromyalgia. Additionally, it could aid in alleviating discomfort in the neck and lower back. The researchers' findings indicate that acupuncture represents a significant alternative therapeutic modality due to its minimal adverse impacts and cost-effectiveness.

In addition, acupuncture has the potential to assist with:

- Hot flashes.
- Nausea.
- Cancer-related fatigue.
- Manifestations of allergic rhinitis.
- Recurring allergy symptoms.

In addition, it is worth noting that a comprehensive meta-analysis conducted on a substantial population of 17,922 patients has demonstrated the efficacy of acupuncture in alleviating chronic pain. Consequently, this therapeutic modality can be considered a suitable option for referrals.

- Outlook

The majority of individuals can be assured of their safety when receiving energy therapy from seasoned practitioners. A prospective practitioner could be reached out to for the purpose of inquiring and engaging in a conversation regarding treatment goals. Additionally, they may acquire further information regarding a practitioner's education and professional background.

Nevertheless, prior to embarking on any novel therapeutic approach, it is advisable for an individual to seek guidance from a qualified healthcare professional, especially if it is intended to complement their existing treatment regimen. Regardless of an individual's pregnancy status, substance usage, or medical conditions, it is advisable for them to consider the potential benefits of engaging in alternative therapeutic approaches, such as energy therapy, in order to determine the suitability of such treatments for their well-being. Energy treatments should not be employed as the solitary remedy for severe or life-threatening symptoms or diseases.

Healing Tools

Throughout the annals of time, individuals have utilized therapeutic implements. The restorative qualities inherent in plants, minerals, and metals rendered them invaluable assets within the medicinal arsenal of ancient shamans, healers, midwives, and practitioners of traditional medicine. Sound has been employed for therapeutic purposes, and modern advancements in technology have considerably enhanced the accessibility of these and other modalities of healing. Healing jewelry, wands, music, and tuning forks represent only a subset of the wide range of therapeutic instruments and implements currently accessible.

What is the objective behind this therapeutic intervention?

Energy therapy aims to promote the unobstructed flow of energy. Individuals may employ it for the purpose of alleviating a specific ailment or enhancing their general state of wellness, with certain individuals opting to integrate it with complementary modalities of energy-based therapies. Energy therapy sessions are frequently provided in establishments focusing on massage and wellness, as well as in conventional medical venues like hospitals and clinics.

"Energy therapy is frequently employed by individuals to address the following conditions:

- Sleep problems.

- The process of wound healing, along with complications related to blood pressure.

- Rheumatoid arthritis.

- Fear and depression.

- Stress.

- Anxiety.

- Pain.

- Migraine.

- Nausea and vomiting.

- Exhaustion.

Rudraksha malas are regarded as power beads believed to possess healing attributes. The rudraksha tree is a perennial plant indigenous to Asia. The fruit yields a bead that has been utilized in adornments and is believed to grant serenity, focus, and safeguard to its wearer. Monks and yogis in India hold the belief that the rudraksha bead symbolizes the underlying nature of the deity Shiva and possesses profound spiritual attributes.

Certain minerals possess traits that render them valuable for the purpose of promoting healing. For centuries, copper has been acknowledged for its therapeutic attributes, and copper bracelets remain prevalent as healing instruments in contemporary times, owing to the metal's inherent anti-inflammatory characteristics. Numerous individuals suffering from arthritis adorn themselves with copper jewelry, affirming its efficacy in reducing pain and swelling. However, it is worth noting that the utilization of copper for therapeutic purposes extends beyond its anti-inflammatory attributes. Copper can also provide internal benefits when ingested. According to research findings, copper has been demonstrated to reduce the probability of ulcers resulting from the usage of anti-inflammatory medications. Additionally, internal administration of copper aids in the healing process of stomach sores.

Copper also exhibits excellent conductivity, rendering it a suitable substance for crafting healing wands. Numerous individuals hold the belief that the combination of copper with diverse crystals and stones in the creation of wands results in potent instruments of healing.

Tuning forks can be considered as an additional therapeutic apparatus. Each tuning fork is indicative of a specific musical note. There are certain individuals who hold the belief that striking two tuning forks together has the potential to bring about alterations in the human body. This unadulterated sound has the potential to instantaneously evoke a feeling of tranquility within individuals, aiding them in attaining a state of emotional balance. Tuning forks are frequently employed in tandem with complementary healing practices like reiki, massage therapy, and yoga.

Music can serve as a modality for healing as well. Certain artists have honed their craft in producing music with rejuvenating properties, and engaging in the act of listening to such music can offer a multitude of therapeutic benefits. Music possesses the capability to alleviate stress and foster a state of heightened focus. The combination of music and subliminal messages is frequently utilized to effectively achieve specific goals, such as the reduction of weight, enhancement of self-assurance, or the pursuit of a compatible life partner.

Achieving A Favorable Mental State

One additional aspect of the creative visualization process involves acquiring the ability to have faith in the present existence of your desired outcome.

This does not pertain to indulging in unrealistic beliefs or compromising one's authenticity. It pertains to the acknowledgment of the veracity entailed in the act of shaping reality, accompanied by a type of unwavering conviction that constitutes the substantiation of intangible phenomena.

Your Mindset

Included in the act of belief is the earnest acquisition of knowledge, whereby one genuinely grasps a certain truth or proposition. It relieves one's burden of contemplation. If you possess unwavering confidence that your intent is fully present in your current circumstances, there is no need to dwell in a state of anticipation or uncertainty regarding its whereabouts, as you already possess it. In the course of your sessions dedicated to visualization, it is imperative to have faith in the fact that you possess what you desire by envisioning yourself thoroughly immersed in the actual act of making the preferred selection.

The teachings of Jesus impeccably encapsulate the fundamental principles of faith: "Whatever you ask for in prayer, believe that you have received it, and it will be yours" (Mark 11:24).

Have faith in your possession of them, and they shall be yours. That constitutes the straightforward process.

Allow me to elucidate on the methods of achieving a suitable mental state and fostering the belief: Engage in a state of relaxation by employing the techniques provided below.

Locate a tranquil environment where you can ensure uninterrupted privacy for a minimum duration of thirty minutes. Please assume an upright position in a comfortable chair, ensuring that both feet are planted firmly on the ground, your back is adequately supported, and your hands are placed gently in your lap. If you so desire, you have the option of reclining, provided that you can ensure you remain awake throughout the entirety of the procedure.

Please shut your eyes and engage in 3 to 5 deep inhalations originating from the abdominal region. Inhale profoundly and consistently through your nostrils, allowing your abdomen to gently elevate or protrude. This exercise promotes diaphragmatic relaxation, facilitating increased air intake into the lungs. Take a brief pause without inhaling and proceed to exhale gradually through your mouth, allowing your abdominal region to naturally relax to its original state.

To ensure proper utilization of appropriate breathing methods, position your hand on your abdomen and engage in practicing this particular form of respiration. This constitutes the correct method of respiratory practice. Develop the ability to breathe in this manner effortlessly during your visualization sessions.

Engage in a deliberate mental countdown, starting from twenty-five and gradually decreasing until you reach one, all the while maintaining consistent deep breaths. In the event that you find that the act of counting backwards fails to induce a state of relaxation, it is advisable to consider commencing the counting process from the number fifty or any number of higher value, as required. Similarly, through consistent practice, you may ascertain that utilizing a countdown method as modest as commencing from ten would suffice for achieving an equivalent level of relaxation.

Subsequently, endeavor to contemplate a tangible aspect in your possession that is undoubtedly assured, such as the shelter that encompasses you, your visual acuity, your motor vehicle, or even the knowledge of a dependable source of income in the near future. Take note of the manner in which your body and mind respond to the presence of something with such unwavering assurance. It is highly probable that you will experience a complete absence of tension, strain, worry, uncertainty, and longing, instead encountering a sense of peace and tranquility that arises from possessing knowledge Grant yourself the opportunity to fully immerse yourself in the state of comprehending the true essence of owning something. Engage in consistent practice of this exercise, and in due course, you will acquire the knowledge of how to believe. Consequently, you will possess the capability to replicate and impart the sensation of trust onto the elements you aim to encounter throughout your sessions of visualization.

In this context, you have acquired knowledge regarding the manner in which your system operates when it possesses a particular element.

With this acquired understanding, one can ascertain whether the current state of their system aligns with the envisioned outcome of their forthcoming session.

Honor Will Guide You To A Position Of Influence

Believers of the Christian faith across the globe are earnestly seeking the divine presence of God both in their religious assemblies and in their personal lives. However, it has come to our attention that there is a growing trend among Christians wherein their faith and trust in God is diminishing, leading them to inquire about the timing of the fulfillment of God's complete blessings in their lives. Taking this into consideration, I have made the decision to introduce an additional indispensable factor that can facilitate a profound encounter with the complete majesty of the divine.

In the professional sphere, esteemed executives are accorded utmost reverence and regard, encapsulating the essence of honor. Honor is an essential and indispensable attribute that can render an individual worthy of hosting the divine presence in their existence. It is an inherent principle that the absence of acknowledgment prevents one from drawing it towards oneself. It is possible that you may not perceive the significance of it. However, I must also assert that the principles of attracting abundance in one's life are closely tied to the ability to appreciate and pay homage to that which is deserving of respect. Additionally, it can be asserted that honor plays an essential role in garnering positive responses and benevolence from individuals whom we hold in high regard.

The aforementioned principle of honor holds true, thereby indicating that when a devout individual makes the choice to pay reverence to the sacred presence of the divine. God will also choose to approach that individual. If a parent is able to demonstrate affection towards a child who reciprocates it with respect, it stands to reason that God, too, will extend compassion and benevolence to those who show Him reverence by approaching Him. This is quite extraordinary, as it suggests that the presence of God can be drawn in by means other than prayer alone. Direct your attention to this profound veracity that I wish to impart upon you. As you have made the conscious choice to bestow reverence upon God, it is imperative that you also hold in high regard the manifestations of the Holy Spirit, whose divine gifts you earnestly seek. Rest assured, without any procrastination, you will soon witness these gifts materialize within your ministry.

By bestowing public or private recognition upon the ordained representatives of the divine, you shall position yourself to partake in the bestowed consecration that graces their existence. Should you choose to pay homage to the magnificence of God in your life and vocation, I can unequivocally assure you that God will bestow upon you the privilege of being immersed in his power, capabilities, jurisdiction, and divine favor. Divine intervention collaborates with mankind, and ultimately, upon the culmination of events, credit shall be rightfully attributed to the supreme force for the accomplishments attained. This is the modus operandi within the divine economy, so it is imperative that we utilize the key of wisdom in order to secure a more favorable and prosperous period in communion with God.

Please refer to Deuteronomy 5:16, whereby it is instructed that one should hold their father and mother in high esteem, in accordance with the divine commandments bestowed upon them by the LORD their God. By doing so, they ensure the prospect of prolonged days and favorable outcomes within the promised land bestowed upon them by the LORD their God. (KJV)

A thorough analysis of the Scriptures indicates that honor holds significant importance as a crucial tool within the realm of God's kingdom. He imparted the commandment unto the prophet Moses, directing him to convey to the congregation of Israel the importance of instructing their offspring to exhibit reverence, esteem, and commemoration towards their parental figures. Never let pride consume you to the extent that you engage in disparaging remarks towards your parents, particularly your father and mother. While you may perceive it differently, it is important to acknowledge that according to sacred scripture, engaging in such behavior is regarded as a transgression against God. Consequently, it has the potential to incur negative repercussions or divine retribution upon those who exhibit such misconduct. This precept is accompanied by a pledge, which I firmly hold to be true. Divine decree has been established by the higher authority to facilitate our recognition of God as our paternal figure. If you encounter challenges in demonstrating reverence towards your father or mother, do you not perceive that it will likely prove challenging to accord reverence to God, who is an unseen Father? If one fails to demonstrate respect towards visible individuals, what assurance can we have of their ability to display reverence towards the imperceptible entities. Therefore, the measure of your integrity towards both mankind and the divine will serve as a criterion for evaluating the extent of the spiritual empowerment bestowed upon you. Exercise prudence, and you shall receive abundant blessings.

Psalm 1:1 states that the individual who refrains from seeking guidance from those who lack religious devotion, avoids accompanying those who engage in sinful behavior, and abstains from associating with those who demonstrate contemptuous attitudes is considered blessed. (KJV)

In previous times, mankind remained unfamiliar with the divine teachings, yet as humanity progressed, the celestial Father graciously ordained certain individuals, through His divine spirit, to receive divine revelations and insights pertaining to His intentions and the welfare of humanity. Those entrusted with the revelation of divine wisdom were obligated to meticulously

transcribe the sacred teachings for the benefit of subsequent eras.
Consequently, the Bible has emerged as the definitive text enabling one to comprehend the divine intention, thereby fostering a conscientious journey alongside God.

The scripture has unequivocally elucidated God's intentions to those who profess their faith in the Lord. I would like to express that by adhering to the guidance outlined in the scripture and striving to align our actions with the divine plan, we aim to avoid causing any distress or disappointment to our Creator. Such behavior will be recognized by God as a commendable display of reverence towards Him. Revolt is a prevalent aspect of human nature. Despite the clear intent of legislation to establish societal norms, it is disconcerting to observe the persistent violation of laws by individuals on a regular basis.

The divine entity seeks not to exert dominion over humanity. He anticipates that we will reach a stage where we will demonstrate our respect and devotion to Him, whether we are being closely monitored or not. It requires a deep sense of devotion and integrity to adhere to the directives and principles of a leader who is no longer present. This poses challenges for individuals of a non-innate disposition. However, in light of our new status as children of God, it is imperative that we acquire the ability to express affection towards our divine Creator. Upon comprehending the concepts of God's omnipresence and omniscience, along with our unwavering conviction that He remains constantly by our side, we shall ultimately attain a higher level of awareness regarding the proper manner in which we ought to serve Him.

It is imperative that we demonstrate our devotion to the Lord by faithfully adhering to His teachings. We are required to refrain from actions that cause him harm, as God possesses a profound sensitivity towards emotions and does not assert his authority upon us. Hence, it is crucial that we demonstrate reverence towards God by upholding his teachings. This is crucial for our advancement and attainment of excellence in the intricacies of our ministerial duties. Adhere to the teachings and precepts of the divine and you will witness a remarkable manifestation of spiritual authority and empowerment in your existence. Obedience is the pathway to your actualization, therefore, do not deviate from your commitment to God. Show reverence to him and you will behold the manifestation of his splendor.

Know Your Objective

It is essential to possess a clear understanding of your objectives and the underlying motivations behind your actions, as this knowledge is crucial for maintaining focus and achieving your desired outcomes. Without a firm grasp on your objectives, you will likely encounter repeated failures in your pursuit of success. Please be advised that the process of materializing one's envisioned outcomes can be challenging. Therefore, in order to attain success, it is imperative to establish your desired objectives in advance.

Establishing your intention is of utmost importance as it can serve as a compass or prompt to articulate your true aspirations in life. If one is uncertain about their desired outcomes in both personal and professional spheres, it is advisable to commence by discerning their goals and objectives. If you have any objectives in mind, compile a roster and ensure its proximity to you. You are free to pursue any aspirations within the confines of your capabilities.

Your intentions will also determine the necessary resources to remain focused on achieving your objectives. If you are still uncertain regarding your objectives, proceed with caution and refrain from hastily establishing your goals. The rationale behind this is that there is a possibility of becoming excessively fixated on a certain aspect, thereby neglecting other necessary items that may be crucial throughout the procedure. It is imperative to consider that effectively evaluating all of your alternatives could present challenges. Engaging in such behavior could potentially lead to confusion and hinder the attainment of the desired outcomes.

Please include solely the essential items that will facilitate the development of your objectives. Eliminate any intentions that you perceive as potentially compromising your goals. Formulating objectives in a joint manner, rather than individually, is recommended, as it is unlikely to yield the desired outcomes. Devote complete focus to your genuine aspirations, while dismissing anything that does not yield any advantages.

When you wish to manifest something, faith will be your energy. Failure to undertake this action will invariably preclude you from attaining the pinnacle of success, thereby depriving you of the desired outcomes. Regrettably, only a limited number of individuals possess an abundance of energy within their physiological composition, as many others persistently permit the intrusion of negative thoughts into their cognitive realm.

If you have encountered difficulties in recent years, it is likely that you have placed your trust in faith. However, individuals who are engaging in manifestation for the first time might encounter difficulties in cultivating profound levels of belief.

It is imperative for all individuals to have faith in their own abilities and potentials. Nevertheless, there are individuals who may lack the knowledge and coping skills to effectively utilize this technique amidst challenging situations, as their responses may be influenced by the circumstances they find themselves in. There exists a multitude of factors that contribute to individuals encountering difficulties in their practice of religion. One of the rationales behind this perspective is that individuals held the belief that by sustaining optimism and maintaining faith in eventual positive outcomes, circumstances would progressively deteriorate.

A prevailing perspective maintains that the preservation of one's faith can be viewed as a valuable attribute, as the susceptibility of individuals to succumb to temptations and harbor pessimistic thoughts is a seemingly pervasive inclination. There are individuals who argue that people are susceptible to the phenomenon known as "shiny object syndrome" due to the belief that acquiring a particular item would substantially alter their circumstances and comprehensively address all their challenges.

Temptation is an inherent element of human existence. Nonetheless, it is crucial to acquire the ability to withstand temptations and fully leverage your faith, as it possesses the capability to propel you in any direction and facilitate your continuous progress.

Possessing faith is akin to possessing a powerful instrument that can be readily deployed in instances where life presents unexpected challenges.

With unwavering conviction, the concept of impossibility will perpetually elude your vocabulary, and any outcomes that may dishearten others shall not deter you, as you remain steadfast in the knowledge that future endeavors shall be executed flawlessly.

The majority of you are likely cognizant of the arduous nature of manifesting one's true desires. However, should you persevere in upholding your faith, you shall imbue yourself with a reservoir of positive energy, thereby expediting the attainment of whatever it is you desire.

Nevertheless, how can one enhance their faith? Developing one's trust can prove to be a challenging undertaking. It is, however, attainable for you to achieve success. Certain individuals demonstrate a commitment to bolstering their beliefs by exerting the necessary endeavors. Enhancing one's religious beliefs does not necessitate adherence to a particular faith or possessing saintly qualities.

You simply need to have faith in your ability to accomplish your objectives. There exists a misconception among certain individuals regarding the concept of enhancing faith, as they erroneously associate faith with religious devotion. It is a possibility, contingent upon the capabilities of the individual. Consequently, the approach one adopts might vary depending on their personal convictions.

Creating A Solid Oneness

We have consistently discussed the concept of unity, and it is now incumbent upon us to delve into the methods by which this collective ideal can be realized. In fact, any approach that facilitates proximity to one's source of power within the universe will engender this unity; however, a significant number of individuals lack the requisite understanding regarding the initial steps to undertake. Consequently, we shall delve into several renowned techniques, which you may endeavor at your discretion until you ascertain the most suitable approach for your needs.

The paramount factor in establishing this connection lies in the capacity to declutter one's thoughts. In the contemporary era characterized by advanced electronics and hectic daily routines, it proves arduous to allocate time for mental repose and liberation from the pressures of daily existence. That is precisely the course of action you must undertake should you aspire to establish any form of rapport with the encompassing cosmos. Spending a moment, let alone a prolonged duration, without any ruminations bustling within the confines of one's mind presents a substantial challenge that surpasses initial perceptions. Through diligent practice and unwavering patience, you will discover that as you cultivate a state of serene tranquility, you can establish a profound communion with the boundless cosmos, transcending the tumultuous nature of existence and diminishing its grip on your being. Through this state of unity, your life will undergo transformation and enhancement. When one can fully embrace the present moment purely for the purpose of existing, without any ulterior motives besides embracing one's true self and current circumstances, an unparalleled sense of peace and serenity is attained.

Prayer is widely recognized among numerous individuals. It is irrelevant which religious affiliation you profess; the act of manifesting is independent of religious beliefs. It represents a profound spiritual realization that facilitates a connection with a transcendent power that transcends physical limitations and is independent of any physical edifice. If one is receptive to the notion of prayer, it serves as a suitable starting point; however, it should not be regarded as the ultimate culmination of one's endeavors. Conventional prayer typically involves expressing gratitude and making requests, yet it typically does not emphasize fostering a closer connection with the divine entity being petitioned. If such were the case, the act of manifesting would be rendered unnecessary as your necessities would already be fulfilled. Nevertheless, one can employ the notion of prayer to gain insight into the mechanics of manifestation in the initial stages of engagement. The fundamental contrast lies in prayer, where conventional teachings have ingrained the belief that individuals are inherently humble beings, unworthy of any blessings, and thus must humbly beseech a higher authority for their desires, given their perceived undeserving nature. Engaging in conventional forms of prayer alone does not suffice to attain a state of unity with one's higher power; rather, it merely serves as a preliminary means to approach such a goal.

Another approach that can be employed is the act of visualizing. If the inescapable presence of visual and auditory disturbances within the environment you inhabit prevents you from locating a serene and undisturbed haven to establish a spiritual connection with the universe, you may direct your focus inwardly to the mental representation of your ideal sanctuary. This skill requires dedicated practice; however, its valuable applications extend beyond mere manifestation, making the effort truly worthwhile. Kindly, shut your eyes and envision the utmost serene location in your thoughts. Indulge in the serene tranquility of the environment you establish. Inhale and exhale at a measured pace, allowing your breath to fully fill your lungs, while embracing a state of calmness and tranquility. Please feel free to take all the necessary time to thoroughly immerse yourself in the mental landscape you have crafted. However, if there is a concern that you might become deeply entranced and be unwilling to depart from this imaginary realm, it may be advisable to establish boundaries in order to regulate your duration of engagement. These boundaries can be implemented through external means, such as utilizing an alarm clock or timer, or through internal mechanisms within your visualization, for instance, by summoning a symbolic entity, be it an animal or an individual, who will indicate when it is time to conclude your reverie and return to reality. Once you have established a serene ambiance within yourself, conducive to relaxation, proceed to connect with the universe and express your desire to align and merge with it. It is advisable to refrain from engaging in such activities while driving or performing any task that demands focus, as there is a possibility of experiencing a lapse in time perception.

This leads us to an important observation: It is mankind who devised and currently finds themselves in servitude to the construct of time. The universe is of eternal existence, transcending the limitations of human comprehension, devoid of any temporal construct as perceived by mankind. Animals possess a distinct perception of time that diverges from that of humans. Animals are guided by their innate survival instincts rather than the reliance on specific temporal cues or the ringing of an alarm. The notion of time is an invention of humanity that presents constant challenges in our day-to-day lives, often leaving us yearning for the ability to halt its unstoppable progression. Indeed, it is possible for you to suspend the passage of time. By refraining from relinquishing control of your life to the passage of time, you will discover an enhanced capacity to experience and capitalize on the opportunities presented to you. It may not be within your immediate reach, neither in the present nor in the near future, but it can be an objective you aspire to and potentially a subject of inquiry that you beseech the cosmos for assistance in comprehending. Consult an individual who is retired, and they will likely express that their perception of time undergoes a significant shift once they are freed from the constraints of work timetables and the expectations imposed by a society governed by strict schedules.

An excellent approach to attaining mental clarity is undeniably through the practice of meditation. There exist a plethora of meditation techniques, all of which are deemed acceptable as long as they effectively facilitate the desired outcome of cultivating a state of mental clarity. Fundamentally, meditation entails the cultivation of concentration skills. Irrespective of whether the target of your attention is your physical self or an external entity, the objective is to attain a state of relaxation and mental clarity by deliberately emptying your mind of all cognitive processes and fixating solely on a single stimulus. Extensive documentation exists showing that the practice of meditation is beneficial in enhancing concentration, fostering feelings of happiness, and reducing levels of stress and anxiety. For individuals unfamiliar with the concept, the most effective approach to initiating the practice of meditation involves selecting a designated time, preferably twice a day as suggested, during which interruptions are avoided. While the majority of individuals tend to opt for a seated position, meditation can be practiced in various postures, such as reclining in a supine position on the floor or ground, depending on one's personal comfort. It is advisable to initiate the session by engaging in controlled muscle stretches, which promote muscle relaxation and help redirect your attention inward. Assume a seated or reclined position and commence by inhaling and exhaling deeply and at a leisurely pace. Moreover, this induces additional muscle relaxation, decreases heart rate, and facilitates enhanced mental concentration. In instances where your mind begins to divert from the present task, simply redirect your attention towards your breathing and the sensations within your body. It may be necessary to repetitively engage in this activity initially, until your mental faculties become accustomed to the notion of taking a respite. If you continue to encounter challenges, it may be beneficial to identify an object to concentrate on (candles tend to have a calming influence on the majority of individuals). Meditation entails the deliberate cultivation of mental relaxation and heightened body awareness, which often surpasses the regular level of attentiveness individuals allocate for such introspection. After establishing a regular pattern and acquiring the capacity to attain a tranquil mental state, one can subsequently prepare oneself to harmonize with the cosmos in a state of unity. Once more, temporality is nonexistent within this state of consciousness. Find tranquility within and allow yourself to unwind. Should any disruptive thoughts arise that disturb your tranquility, it is important to acknowledge their existence and subsequently dismiss them through the process of redirecting your attention towards your chosen focal point, be it the act of breathing, the sensations within your body, or an external object.

Numerous individuals attest to engaging in meditation as a means to address unresolved challenges, wherein the subsequent practice of meditation often leads to a profound internal realization and revelation of solutions. On certain occasions, the solutions to the challenges we face are inherently within us. However, the disorder or tumult prevailing in our lives often hinders us from perceiving these solutions with utmost clarity. The aforementioned adage "consider overnight" exhibits similar validity in this context. If the brain is afforded the opportunity to decelerate and methodically process the necessary information rather than being constantly bombarded with every trivial piece of data that permeates our lives, then the mind becomes an exceptionally potent instrument. The detachment of the conscious thought process and the subconscious thought process enables the mind to attain a state of liberation, enabling it to establish a connection with the unity of the universe. The insights gained from this connection are typically disregarded as mere coincidences. We inadvertently neglect to acknowledge the appropriate recognition in such instances.

At times, it is necessary for us to simply decelerate and allow the universe to gently make its presence known to us. Allocate a brief portion of your time in an outdoor setting observing the fauna, and you shall be astounded by the profound immediacy with which the surrounding natural environment operates. We, as human beings, have become disengaged with the vastness of the universe in which we exist. Due to the remarkable capabilities of our minds in processing vast amounts of information, we have inadvertently disconnected ourselves from the fundamental origin of our existence, resulting in our own discontentment. We harbor concerns regarding various aspects of our lives, encompassing matters such as sustenance and attire, the selection of companions, and the determination of our place of residence. Both animals and plants are devoid of such concerns, despite being crafted by the same omnipotent creator.

Discover a location that affords the opportunity to observe and potentially engage with the natural environment. Remain in a composed posture, engage in deliberate and measured respiration, and attentively perceive the natural auditory stimuli. There exists a state of tranquility encompassing our surroundings, provided that we are open to its influence. Embedded within that state of tranquility exists a profound sense of unity with the cosmic order. It permeates our daily existence, yet we must actively strive to engage with it, possess the earnest aspiration to harness that connection, and ardently seek its potential for the collective well-being of all living entities. Merely because it is present in the world does not imply that it will actively seek your attention and require you to acknowledge it accordingly. In order for any progress to occur, you must direct your attention towards it and cultivate a genuine aspiration for its establishment. In order to achieve this, it is imperative to possess a clear and unburdened mind, free from a lengthy inventory of tasks or the encumbrance of electronic devices. It is challenging to direct one's attention towards emptiness when our lives are replete with abundance. The majority of individuals struggle significantly with the task of remaining immobile and engaged in idleness for a complete duration of ten minutes. Throughout the span of ten minutes, your cognitive processes will traverse every conceivable thought, including those tasks you ought to undertake, concurrently hindering your capacity to establish and foster a harmonious relationship with the cosmos surrounding you.

Grant yourself the liberty to temporarily withdraw from the mundane concerns and tensions of your daily life. It will remain accessible to you, whether in ten minutes or even an hour from now. To effectively aspire for a more promising future, it is imperative that you allocate yourself sufficient time for the purposeful cultivation of manifestation skills. Ultimately, similar to all aspects of existence, accomplishing anything of value necessitates the exertion of effort on your behalf.

Have A Clear Understanding Of Your Desires And Make A Conscious Request To The Universe

Regardless of whether you find yourself trapped in an undesirable job or an unfulfilling relationship, the reason behind your dissatisfaction can be traced back to a lack of initial clarity and unwavering determination in embarking on your path. Regrettably, such is the modus operandi for the majority of individuals, thereby resulting in a perpetual state of discontentment with regards to our lives overall and any significant facets thereof.

As previously mentioned, we possess the ability to shape our reality through our choices and actions in all aspects of our existence. Our cognition dictates our emotions, our emotions exert an impact on our behaviors, and our behaviors consequently mold our perceived truth. To regain control over your life and make your heartfelt aspirations a reality, it is imperative that you attain a comprehensive understanding of your desires and explicitly manifest these intentions to the universe, abstaining from requesting any undesired outcomes.

Ensure clarity regarding your desires

When you have complete clarity on what you want, you are able to put out those crystal clear intentions out in the universe and draw towards you all the people, resources, help, assistance and opportunities required to translate them into reality.

If you have previously attended Tony Robbins' lectures and podcasts on self-improvement, you would likely be familiar with his belief in the necessity of complete clarity in order to effectively harness the power of the Law of Attraction. During one of his presentations, Robbin explicitly articulates the notion that being unclear about your desires will invariably result in failure to attain them. If your sole objective is to acquire monetary wealth, without a clear understanding of how much is required, you will perpetually find yourself unsatisfied with the wealth that you attain. You might experience an increase in your weekly earnings by $100 compared to your previous income, or you might secure a job that offers a salary five times higher than your previous employment. Despite these financial advancements, your discontentment would persist. This occurrence arises due to the absence of desired outcomes being met, which can be solely attributed to a lack of lucidity in defining one's intentions.

On a daily basis, you consistently transmit numerous thoughts into the cosmos, and frequently, the majority of these thoughts exhibit a considerable lack of specificity. They consistently fail to provide precise specifications regarding your desired outcome, thereby only offering fragments and glimpses rather than a comprehensive solution. It is imperative that you allocate your undivided attention, steadfast concentration, unwavering determination, and lucidity towards your desired objectives, as this is the only way to attain them.

Request Your Desires from the Cosmos

Once you have obtained clarity regarding your desires, it is imperative to actively pursue the fulfillment of those specific needs through seeking assistance from the universe. Frequently, rather than expressing our desires directly, we tend to outline the aspects we find undesirable and subsequently experience lamentation over the incongruity between our envisioned life and our present reality. Rather than expressing a desire for wealth, one may assert a preference for avoiding poverty. Instead of centering on the pursuit of a soul mate, one might prioritize methods for not eliciting the attention of unsuitable individuals.

One issue that pervades many individuals is their tendency to fixate on misguided priorities and remain oblivious to the intricacies of cognitive processes. The human cognitive processes fail to discern between the boundaries of reality and imagination, while also exhibiting an inability to comprehend expressions imbued with negative undertones. This implies two key aspects:-

a) It prioritizes and embraces any suggestions with unwavering faith. If one continues to dwell upon the potential outcome of losing a tennis match against their employer, or the risk of being terminated from their position due to a significant error, it is inevitable that they will ultimately experience defeat in both the match and the realm of employment. Nevertheless, should you choose to realign your focus and diligently strategize on how to emerge victorious in the competition, as well as mitigate the impact of your error on your professional standing, you will ultimately uncover a pathway to attaining your objectives. That which you concentrate on with profound conviction, the cosmos aids you in achieving. In order for this to occur, it is imperative that you maintain a steadfast concentration, as your subconscious mind readily assimilates all the notions you impart to it. In order for you to achieve success, it is imperative that you provide it with the accurate information.

b) The suggestion selectively excludes all words that convey a negative connotation. Regrettably, our minds appear to have difficulty comprehending the negations expressed by words such as 'no', 'never', and 'don't'. If you fail to comprehend this concept, contemplate a time in your past where you were explicitly instructed not to engage in a certain action, yet you disregarded those instructions. This could be refraining from consuming chocolate cake due to being on a dietary regimen or abstaining from staying out late with friends. In instances where you are instructed to refrain from a certain action, an overwhelming inclination arises within you to partake in said action, ultimately resulting in active participation. This phenomenon occurs due to the cognitive limitation of the mind to assimilate and integrate the concept of negation, prompting it to disregard the "no" element within the suggestion and subsequently modify its content. "I will engage in the consumption of cake" transforms into "I will partake in the consumption of cake," while "I will not arrive at the workplace tardy" shifts to "I will arrive at the workplace tardy." It is imperative to direct your attention towards your desires rather than negate them, in order to properly transmit the intended message into the universe.

Now that you have acquired an understanding of the scientific principles underlying the necessity of having a clear understanding of your desires and objectives, allow me to present the means by which you can achieve such clarity to petition the universe exclusively for the appropriate manifestations.

How to Manifest Your Deepest Desires Through the Power of Intention

Presented herein is a systematic and straightforward methodology that may aid one in achieving clarity regarding their desires, allowing for the utilization of the universal forces to manifest said desires.

Find a serene location, take out your diary, and contemplate your profound aspirations. To facilitate comprehension, consider focusing on the particular aspect of your life that gives you the greatest level of concern. It encompasses various aspects, including one's physical well-being, financial prosperity, emotional contentment, romantic relationships, professional achievements, and more.

One approach to accomplish this task would be to generate a set of columns corresponding to the primary facets of your life, and subsequently delineate each of these domains in a comprehensive manner, one by one. Consider the existing condition and state of each area, and evaluate your level of satisfaction with them. As an illustration, in the event that an individual exceeds their optimal weight by 50 pounds and begins to experience adverse health effects like diabetes, it may be safe to assume that such outcomes are not aligned with their health objectives.

After meticulously outlining the aspects of a particular area that you find unfavorable, consider forming a clear vision of your desired outcome and proceed to provide a comprehensive description of it. Consider the desires you held in your youth, those that yield utmost delight, those that have escaped your grasp, those that compel admiration towards others, and the similar. Make an effort to align with the sentiments and thoughts emanating from your inner self, establishing a connection with both aspects and directing your attention towards genuine aspirations harbored within your heart.

Once you have come across something, diligently examine it and thoroughly analyze it from various perspectives in order to attain a comprehensive understanding of your objectives. If you perceive wealth as your ultimate necessity, refrain from merely accepting this notion as is, but rather strive to refine and articulate this imperative need with utmost precision. Consider the precise quantity of wealth that you require and seek out a figure that would adequately fulfill your desires. Should you desire a sum of one million, I suggest articulating this clearly in writing. Alternatively, if a lesser amount, such as $50,000, would satisfy you, that could serve as your designated level of prosperity. In the pursuit of finding a suitable companion, it is advisable to articulate the qualities and attributes desired in a partner, rather than settling for the vague term of a 'soul mate'. Bearing in mind that precision enhances the efficacy of communication with the cosmic forces, it will significantly contribute to the realization of one's desired objective.

It is permissible to devote several days or even weeks to attaining absolute clarity regarding your desires, for it is only when you possess a distinct understanding of your authentic requirements that you can envision and have unwavering faith in the realization of such aspirations. Therefore, it is advised to allocate sufficient time for that particular task in order to subsequently select the appropriate course of action for reaching your intended goal. Your subsequent course of action entails embracing both your personal capabilities and the immense potential of the cosmos, while fostering ambitious aspirations.

Losing Gracefully

An individual who possesses a genuine sense of achievement will comprehend that it is impossible to emerge victorious in every endeavor consistently. Regrettably, it is simply unattainable. While they make diligent efforts whenever feasible, it is imperative for them to comprehend and acknowledge that occasional predicaments may arise. On occasion, another individual may surpass one's abilities or aptitude. Occasionally, one may encounter an unfavorable day or encounter that does not meet their expectations. It is an undeniably regrettable circumstance, yet it necessitates one's ability to acknowledge and navigate through it. What are the consequences when one experiences a loss despite being the victor?

It is crucial to exhibit gracefulness. It is imperative to ensure that one maintains a considerate and respectful demeanor towards others, regardless of one's personal emotions. It can be distressing to experience the loss of something one has invested immense passion and effort into. It is imperative to ensure adequate preparedness for this. Consider contingency plans in advance of embarking on a task, as this will ensure the utmost preparedness in the event of failure. While it is certainly important to maintain a belief in oneself and envision victory, it is essential to acknowledge the potential outcome of not achieving the desired result. Ensure that you are adequately equipped with the necessary knowledge and skills to conduct yourself in a courteous manner when the occasion arises.

After experiencing a defeat, it is important to engage in a conversation with the victor. Congratulate them. Ensure that you express your admiration for their exceptional abilities, and ensure that you depart with your dignity preserved. It would be advisable for you to promptly approach and extend your hand in greeting as one of the initial individuals, as this demonstrates your ability to accept defeat graciously. Furthermore, this indicates that you possess commendable virtues. Ultimately, it is conceivable that this outcome might prove equally, if not more, beneficial, as it garners the respect and admiration of others for one's exemplary conduct.

It is of utmost importance to bear this in mind even when you emerge victorious. It is entirely appropriate to feel enthusiastic and express confidence in one's abilities. It is deemed appropriate to declare that your product, cuisine, etc. was the best. It is deemed inappropriate to make any disparaging remarks concerning your competitors. It is imperative to refrain from disparaging a competitor as such actions inevitably reflect poorly upon oneself. Engaging in cruel or rude behavior gives the impression of being a poor sport, both in defeat and in victory, and such conduct is generally frowned upon by others. It has the potential to exert a detrimental impact on your business, as well as implicate your personal reputation.

When one demonstrates the ability to display amicability and courtesy towards individuals, regardless of one's personal opinions towards them or their actions, one is exhibiting the qualities of moral superiority. Observers will perceive such actions and evaluate the justifiability of your behavior towards the individual in question. This will greatly enhance the chances of them seeking your assistance in the future, as they are aware of the quality of your offerings and your reliability as a trustworthy individual.

It is essential to continuously exhibit exemplary behavior without openly flaunting it to others. Please bear in mind that, in order to truly embody the qualities of a morally superior individual, it is essential to demonstrate politeness, empathy, and reverence towards others. Engaging in these activities can pose challenges on occasions when you perceive yourself as a victim of injustice or experience negative sentiments towards another individual. It is imperative that you persist in demonstrating these characteristics and refrain from making derogatory remarks about individuals, even when you possess indisputable evidence of the veracity of a claim. One would not desire to be perceived as 'that individual.'

If one possesses knowledge about another business or individual that has the potential to cause harm, one may perceive it as their duty to disclose said information. If one possesses the ability to convey a cautionary message in a helpful manner, maintaining an amicable and optimistic tone towards others, that would be highly commendable. However, it must be acknowledged that sometimes such capability may not be at our disposal. A champion will always prioritize issuing essential alerts for the safety and welfare of others, even if it means risking damage to their own reputation. Please endeavor to ensure that the information remains strictly factual, providing only information that you possess with complete certainty or genuinely believe to be accurate. In the event that you incorporate subjective viewpoints or deviate excessively from objective information, it could have more adverse consequences for both parties involved. Consequently, the individual you are advising may be less inclined to accept your guidance, as they may perceive it as an afflictive case of displaying unsportsmanlike conduct.

Prosperity

Prosperity should not be solely equated to the possession of financial surplus. Furthermore, one's perspective on life also influences their prosperity. A gentleman may possess substantial wealth and still fail to find genuine happiness or achieve true success, for that matter. The acquisition of wealth does not bring him true happiness. True happiness emanates from an internal source rather than being derived from material possessions. Consequently, it becomes apparent that money cannot be used as a means to attain happiness directly; nevertheless, one can strive to manifest the desired level of financial abundance. Assuming your objective is to accumulate savings of $100 per month; however, presently you are experiencing considerable difficulties in managing your finances. The amount of $100 per month is merely conjectural, however, if one consistently reinforces the notion within oneself: "

I allocate $100 per month towards saving.

You condition your mindset to effectively manifest that goal. You prioritize anchoring your life around the conviction that you are already achieving such monthly savings, rather than perceiving it as a mere endeavor or contingency plan. Adopting the belief that you are already practicing frugality enhances your awareness of your financial situation and instills a definitive objective to exercise self-discipline through minimizing expenditure on non-essential items that do not align with your genuine priorities. An additional consequence of maintaining the belief that you generate, possess, and accumulate a minimum level of income is that you will commence to draw greater financial wealth into your existence. A particular individual whom I assisted in actualizing affluence in his life faced significant challenges in meeting his financial obligations, resorting to requesting payday loans on a weekly basis. He possessed a strong inclination to alter these detrimental financial patterns, and his sole means of accomplishing this feat resided in materializing the desirable prosperity he aspired to attain.

He employed a vision board as a means of visually presenting his financial goals, seeking a sense of financial stability wherein concerns over bills and monetary responsibilities would be alleviated. Upon determining the essential prerequisites, he adeptly orchestrated his lifestyle to align with his ambitions, ultimately surpassing his own anticipated outcomes. Do you believe you have a chance at winning the lottery? Why not? If one possesses unwavering faith in their ability to triumph, they may ultimately evolve into an individual capable of materializing abundance in their existence.

There exist remarkable anecdotal accounts of lottery victories available on YouTube, and the examination of how individuals employed concepts such as manifestation and the Law of Attraction proves highly captivating. A woman possessed precise knowledge of the exact amount of money she was going to acquire. Uncertain of the precise timing, she harbored unwavering faith in her concept, to the extent that she positioned a document beneath her pillow explicitly stating the precise sum she anticipated acquiring. Subsequently, she would gently shut her eyelids, envisioning herself as the fortunate recipient of the aforementioned sum of money. Altering her perspective, she never experienced distress upon the failure of a ticket to win, as she held firm conviction that a significant victory would inevitably materialize.

When it occurred, she indeed attained the precise sum she had been focusing on. Mentally, she displayed unwavering certainty that this outcome was predetermined, not confined to mere fantasies, but rather a tangible reality she was currently experiencing. The magnitude of her favorable energy was such that ultimately, she emerged victorious and her winnings precisely aligned with the amount she had documented on that sheet of paper.

It does not pertain to luck. The individual who tears apart his lottery ticket and perceives himself as a failure often remains unsuccessful throughout his entire existence. Individuals who demonstrate affluence will draw forth the abundance and vitality inherent in monetary resources through the emission of elevated frequency vibrations, representing their positive convictions regarding money and its effortless acquisition. The Law of Attraction diligently ensures the consistent realization of this phenomenon, unfailingly, without exception. The level of difficulty associated with the sacrifices required to attain that goal is quite substantial for numerous individuals. Should you encounter discouragement and lose faith in your aspirations, it is imperative that you reinvigorate your efforts and restart the process. However, maintaining a steadfast belief in your affluence and your ability to effortlessly attract wealth will significantly enhance the likelihood of transforming that notion into a tangible reality.

In order to maintain a constant sense of encouragement through the sustained reinforcement of positive beliefs, it is highly recommended to make a habit of routinely revisiting your vision board at a minimum frequency of twice per day: once upon awakening in the morning, and once prior to retiring for the night. It is imperative for the attainment of success in cultivating positive beliefs that you dedicate time to perusing your vision board prior to retiring for the night. This practice is vital as during sleep, your subconscious mind assumes control and perpetuates the processing of the most recent information assimilated. Furthermore, it is within the depths of your subconscious that all beliefs come to fruition and are retained. Additionally, it is crucial to emphasize that examining your vision board promptly upon awakening serves as an equally vital practice in fortifying these convictions. This is due to the fact that upon emerging from slumber, the conscious mind operates akin to a tabula rasa, making it an ideal opportunity to reinforce positive beliefs. Prior to engaging with your mobile device, attending to text messages, perusing electronic mail, or accessing any informational or societal online platforms, incorporate the practice of reviewing your vision board into your daily morning routine, ensuring optimal prospects for accomplishing desired objectives. This daily analysis will establish the ambiance for the day and encourage a favorable atmosphere.

The energy you emanate is what influences the energy of the Universe, irrespective of its polarity, whether it be positive or negative. The greater the positivity in the energy, the more favorable the outcomes will be. Therefore, it is imperative that you exert maximum effort to elevate your energy levels. In the forthcoming chapter, we shall delve into various methodologies for accomplishing this task. Nevertheless, as evidenced throughout the preceding chapters, it is apparent that one's optimistic disposition and unwavering faith in their aspirations have a paramount influence on the actualization of their dreams, surpassing any other factor within our earthly realm.

A gentleman named Joe expressed a desire to pursue a career as a guitarist. He was 41 years old and had never held a guitar in his life. He acquired knowledge due to its significance in his life and held a strong belief in his own musical abilities. He held the belief that he was, and as such, he successfully achieved his dream. Irrespective of the aspiration at hand, the attainment of your goals is contingent upon the level of energy you possess. Therefore, it is imperative to elevate your energy levels in order to optimize the effectiveness of the Law of Attraction, taking into account your unique circumstances.

Ways To Manifest Greatness

Your thoughts play a pivotal role in shaping the course of your future. Engage in contemplation of your desires until you develop unwavering conviction in them. Once an individual is capable of embracing the belief that their aspirations hold tangible potential and can indeed materialize, they shall witness the manifestation of said aspirations in actuality. Thoughts eventually become things. The circumstances and events that come into your life are aligned with your prevailing thoughts.

Demonstrate immense potential by firmly embracing your capacity to redefine your circumstances. Certainly, achieving greatness will require considerable effort and will not be attained effortlessly. The appearances before you may be misleading and potentially discourage you from pursuing your aspirations and objectives. It is important to bear in mind that you will inevitably face obstacles and your convictions will be subject to scrutiny; however, remain steadfast in your faith and observe as your aspirations effortlessly materialize in the realm of existence.

You possess inherent greatness, and it is incumbent upon you to actualize and demonstrate that greatness.

Presented below are five (5) methods to actualize greatness;

Have faith in the splendor of your aspirations.

All that you are deserving of is steadily advancing towards you. It is imperative to possess a profound conviction in the exquisite nature of your aspirations.

Maintain an unwavering conviction that extraordinary occurrences are on the brink of manifesting. Do not be disheartened by the challenges you face. Proceed with assurance towards the realization of your aspirations.

If you persist in adhering to your conventional patterns of thinking, you will perpetually obtain the same outcomes you have consistently acquired in the past. If you have persistently dwelled upon negative thoughts and experienced a lack of success, why not consider altering your cognitive framework?

Commence embracing the inherent splendor of your aspirations, as they are swiftly approaching actualization, particularly in this current juncture. As per your convictions, you will gradually start discerning indications that your desired outcome is imminent.

Make a practical plan.

In order to achieve greatness, it is imperative to have a strategic plan in place. The absence of strategic planning is tantamount to preparing for failure. The most effective approaches to mental control entail engaging the mind with a well-defined objective, supported by a concrete strategy.

Explore your areas of interest and actively engage yourself in them. One can never hope to actualize significant achievements without the presence of a well-crafted strategy, alongside the requisite diligence and unwavering resolve to execute said plan. The realization of your aspirations and objectives can solely be accomplished through the implementation of a well-founded strategy that garners your utmost conviction, followed by diligent efforts towards their actualization.

A goal lacking a feasible strategy amounts to mere aspirations, devoid of substance. Fortuitous occurrences are non-existent; all events unfold as a result of careful deliberation.

Stay committed.

The attainment of greatness is never facilitated by ease and simplicity. That which is easily attained will not endure, and that which endures will not be easily attained. If one possesses a cherished aspiration, it is imperative to remain firmly dedicated to its pursuit in order for it to materialize in the realm of actuality. Maintain unwavering dedication to your aspirations until they are realized.

Devotion is the pivotal factor in attaining one's aspirations. It may prove more challenging than anticipated. The procedure may entail discomfort and may require a significant amount of time to materialize; however, the ultimate outcome will prove to be worthwhile. Maintain unwavering dedication and exercise self-control in order to meticulously make reasoned choices that will lead to the realization of your aspirations.

If you possess unwavering dedication to your dreams and aspirations, no objective will remain beyond your reach. Maintain unwavering dedication and have faith in your ability to accomplish all that you aspire for. It will pose challenges, yet at an unforeseen moment, you will come to the realization that all your aspirations are materializing.

Exercising patience is fundamental to the realization of desired outcomes.

There are no impediments impeding your access to that which you fervently aspire to attain. If you possess such a mindset, you would display patience in anticipating the realization of your rightful entitlements. Fortuitous circumstances are bestowed upon those who possess unwavering faith, superior opportunities are granted to those who exhibit patience, and the utmost rewards are attained by those who persevere steadfastly without surrendering. Cultivate patience and steadfastly persevere in your pursuit of that which is rightfully yours.

Acquiring the virtue of patience does not imply the necessity to remain inactive or idle. Exercising patience entails consistently striving towards your goals while maintaining a composed demeanor in regard to the outcomes. Acquire the skill of cultivating patience amidst challenging circumstances. Regardless of the adversities encountered in life, it is imperative to maintain composure and forbearance.

By maintaining perseverance throughout the process while steadfastly adhering to your convictions, you will gradually manifest the objects of your desires. Maintain unwavering conviction in your beliefs and do not surrender it through impetuosity. All that you require is readily available, thus displaying a measure of forbearance during the anticipation of their materialization would be advisable.

Always be grateful.

An appreciative heart acts as a catalyst for extraordinary occurrences. Expressing appreciation unlocks the potential for various prospects to manifest themselves in one's life. The multitude of remarkable advantages derived from gratitude outweigh the considerable expense of ingratitude. If one maintains a constant state of gratitude, it is possible to bring forth one's deepest desires. It is crucial to bear in mind that neglecting to show appreciation for the minor blessings bestowed upon you by life may hinder the arrival of significant opportunities in your path. If one lacks fidelity in trivial matters, they shall similarly lack fidelity when entrusted with much greater responsibilities.

Cultivate a sense of gratitude, even in instances where your desires remain unfulfilled. Express gratitude for what you presently possess without harboring complaints concerning the perceived lack of opportunities or possessions. Rest assured, there is no need for concern when life presents you with less than what you rightfully merit. What is destined for you will invariably find its way into your life, therefore, express appreciation for the inconspicuous blessings as they manifest indications that your desired outcome is approaching.

Faith is a prerequisite for the actualization of desired outcomes.

The presence of faith serves as a crucial component in the realization of one's desires, as it embodies the foundation upon which aspirations are built. In the absence of faith, the realization of your aspirations will remain elusive. On certain occasions, it can be challenging to maintain belief amidst a circumstance that appears devoid of any remaining prospects.

Typically, once an individual begins harboring thoughts that they are incapable of overcoming a challenging circumstance, it is often at this juncture that the cosmos presents a symbol or indication. It is possible to bring about whatever you desire through unwavering faith in the belief that all circumstances will ultimately align in your favor. You are in closer proximity to manifesting your desires than you realize, thus it would be prudent to remain attentive to the signs.

Subconscious Goal Programming

One can implant their dreams or aspirations into their subconscious mind by employing techniques such as sensory visualization or positive affirmation.

Sensualization refers to the manifestation of information or concepts through a comprehensive and immersive representation that engages multiple senses. The concept of an effective visualization entails engaging and stimulating all sensory faculties. So it appears that your perception extends beyond imagination to include auditory and tactile experiences as well. Moreover, if necessary, you have the option to utilize your sense of smell and taste as well.

Sensualization needs a scenario. Please provide a comprehensive account of your accomplishments, detailing the events, outcomes, personal encounters, observations, auditory experiences, and emotional responses that occurred upon attaining your objective in a lucid manner. Please record all of it! This scenario represents the imagery that you create in your thoughts when experiencing sensuality.

Affirmation entails expressing a constructive declaration. General affirmation and specific affirmation both constitute two distinct forms of affirmation. The example of general affirmation is "I am a money magnet", while the specific affirmation is "My monthly income is $100,000". It is imperative that both general affirmations and specific affirmations adhere to the criteria of being personal, stated in the present tense, and formulated as positive sentences.

There exist two crucial prerequisites for achieving effective outcomes in sensualization and affirmation.

1. There is an absence of any discomfort.

2. Conducted while in a hypnotic condition.

Initially, there is an absence of any discomfort. What emotions arise when considering your aspirations and ambitions. If you are experiencing positive emotions and are in a favorable state, proceed to the second step. However, should you experience negative emotions or a sense of discomfort, it is imperative that you address and resolve them before moving forward.

In the event that you experience unease or discomfort, it stands to reason that you would refrain from engaging with the situation, would you not? If you possess a height phobia, you will refrain from visiting places at elevated altitudes. Should you experience any discomfort towards your aspirations, it is unlikely that your subconscious mind will be able to attain them.

In essence, the processes of sensualization and affirmation serve as means to implant a novel program into the depths of your subconscious psyche. In the event that a contradictory program resides within your subconscious mind, no matter how many times you engage in the process of visualization and affirmation, the new program will be disregarded. It is imperative to create room within your subconscious mind for the assimilation of a novel program. Prior to proceeding, it is imperative to uninstall any outdated or incompatible software that may be present on your system. One may opt to utilize either the Sedona Method or Ho'oponopono techniques.

Additionally, it is essential to induce a state of heightened sensory perception and assert one's affirmations while under a state of hypnosis. When an individual is under hypnosis, their subconscious mind becomes highly receptive to suggestions, thereby providing an opportunity to deliberately program it according to one's desired outcome.

In the event that you lack knowledge of the techniques for engaging in self-hypnosis or find yourself lacking the time necessary to engage in such practices, alternative options are available in the form of two naturally occurring hypnotic states, specifically referred to as hypnopompic and hypnagogic states.

Hypnopompic refers to the transitional state of awareness that occurs upon awakening from slumber. It occurs briefly during the early hours of awakening.

Hypnagogic represents the intermediary period when shifting from a state of wakefulness to the state of slumber. It occurs for a duration of thirty minutes prior to your slumber in the evening.

Practicing sensualization and affirmation at night is much more effective than practicing it in the morning. There exists a phenomenon known as "The Magic 30 Minutes" or the period thirty minutes prior to the onset of sleep. The actions you take during this period will serve as a catalyst for a significant aspiration. If you were to view a horror film prior to your slumber, it is highly likely that it would infiltrate your dreamscape, resulting in a sinister nocturnal experience. The subconscious realm possesses the ability to employ dreams as a means of communication with individuals. We have allocated a dedicated chapter to address this topic.

In order to derive advantageous outcomes from the process of sensualization and affirmation, it is imperative to bear in mind the following criteria: avoidance of any resulting discomfort and execution thereof in a state of hypnosis.

If you are seeking further knowledge on the topic of self-hypnosis, I would recommend perusing my previous publication, titled "Ultimate Self-Hypnosis for Beginners: Unlock Your Maximum Potential through Self-

Hypnosis Techniques, Irrespective of Your Proficiency in Hypnotic Practices."

Step 4- Alleviate The Effects Of Stress On Your Nerves Through Maintaining A Healthy Diet, Getting Ample Rest, And Engaging In Regular Physical Activity.

In order to achieve a state of genuine inner tranquility, it is imperative to prioritize and devote attention to three fundamental components and requisites of one's life: nutrition, rest, and physical activity. The demanding lifestyle that one leads exacts a physical toll and causes one to neglect these three factors. A hectic lifestyle often leads individuals to neglect proper nutrition, rest, and physical activity.

When one is burdened with a tightly packed agenda, there is a perpetual sense of urgency. You fail to prioritize the consumption of nutritious foods and instead become increasingly reliant on convenience food options. These food items, encompassing carbonated beverages, energy drinks, frozen foods, and unhealthy foods, are replete with processed and artificial components, genetically modified organisms, trans-fats, and LDL (commonly referred to as bad cholesterol.) All of these constituents are acknowledged to elevate cortisol and cholesterol levels within your body, both of which are correlated with heightened levels of stress.

Additionally, an intense schedule frequently results in minimal opportunities for relaxation and rest. After a long and arduous day, you return to your abode only to find yourself in a state of weariness. However, despite your exhaustion, you are compelled to engage in diligent efforts towards a significant project. You persist in laboring late into the night and manage to catch only a few hours of sleep, just to awaken and discover your alarm clock eagerly bouncing about. You rise from your brief respite and depart for your place of employment. Insufficient rest and sleep hinder the body's ability to adequately restore fatigued and overworked muscles. When one's body lacks relaxation, it initiates a state of exhaustion, consequently leading to heightened levels of stress.

If one's schedule does not allow for adequate nutrition and rest, it becomes infeasible to allocate any time for physical fitness. Research has demonstrated that individuals who lead a predominantly inactive lifestyle exhibit a higher susceptibility to stress compared to those who partake in regular physical activity. Conforming to a hectic lifestyle will invariably result in the intrusion of stress into both your body and mind, thereby hindering your ability to achieve your goals. In order to attain a state of calmness, happiness, and serenity, it is imperative that one applies efforts towards addressing these three factors in their life.

Center your efforts on enhancing your dietary habits, optimizing your sleep routine, and cultivating increased physical activity.

Prior to anything else, and of utmost significance, it is imperative that you eliminate all the nutritionally deficient foods from your diet. Commence by gradually incorporating a diverse range of nutritious produce, such as tomatoes, apples, oranges, berries, and leafy greens, into your dietary regimen. These food items are abundant sources of beta-carotenes, lycopene, and various other antioxidants that effectively eliminate free radicals within the body, thus promoting a state of tranquility and vitality. Gradually incorporate fish, dairy, soy products, and nuts into your dietary intake. These foods contain abundant quantities of vitamins A, C, K, E, protein, favorable fats, and calcium, which encompass all the essential nutrients necessary for promoting and maintaining optimal bodily functions. Furthermore, it is imperative to consume a daily amount of two to three liters of water, as this aids in the regulation of your metabolism and sustains a rejuvenated state.

Additionally, it is imperative that you make a conscious effort to prioritize obtaining a minimum of seven to eight uninterrupted hours of sleep during night hours, while also incorporating a brief period of rest or a nap lasting approximately 30 to 40 minutes during daytime. Upon adopting a dietary regimen that emphasizes cleanliness, you will discover an enhanced capacity to attain restful sleep during the evening hours. Proper sleep plays a critical role in modulating stress levels and enhancing cognitive vigor and concentration.

Furthermore, it is imperative that you commence integrating physical activity and exercise into your daily routine. Engage in any form of strenuous physical activity for a minimum duration of 15 minutes on a daily basis and gradually extend this duration to reach an hour. Engaging in physical activity enhances the production of serotonin and dopamine, neurotransmitters associated with augmenting one's mood and psychological state, resulting in reduced stress levels and heightened feelings of tranquility and serenity.

Direct your attention towards implementing these three remarkable and impactful modifications in your life, and within a span of three weeks, you will perceive a significant alleviation of your stress. As the body attains a state of tranquility, the mind concurrently assumes a state of greater serenity, enabling enhanced concentration on the cultivation of constructive thoughts to bring about the fruition of one's objectives.

To achieve success, it is imperative to exhibit uniqueness.
You are subjecting yourself to the disparagement of detractors due to your unique qualities, such as your achievement of success and your innovative thinking. The discrepancy being identified is the very element that is drawing criticism, and paradoxically, the same characteristic that has contributed to your remarkable success. Embrace the reality that your uniqueness sets you apart, distinguishing you from those who have not achieved comparable levels of success.

Below are several characteristics that distinguish successful individuals from the general population:

They exhibit a steadfast commitment to their objectives, directing their attention and efforts towards their intended outcomes, rather than fixating on the obstacles encountered during the journey.

Those who hold negative opinions towards you eagerly anticipate your failure, and it is inevitable that you will encounter obstacles both in your journey towards success and even after achieving it. Success is reserved for individuals who possess the ability to rise from failure, assimilate valuable lessons, and utilize such experiences as driving forces towards further achievements.

Individuals who have achieved success do not actively pursue satisfaction in their lives, as you have already gleaned from the insights presented in chapter 7. Continuously inquire, "What steps shall I take subsequently?" to ensure the continued attainment of triumph. Do not become complacent with your current circumstances.

Difficulties, vexations, and hindrances are regarded merely as minor inconveniences encountered in the pursuit of the ultimate goal. Do not permit them to discourage your motivation; instead, utilize them as a source of inspiration.

Successful individuals hold their dreams in such high regard that they are unaffected by the critiques of detractors or preoccupied with gaining the approval of others.

Although it may be challenging for you to accept negative criticism, you have the opportunity to utilize it for personal growth and to enhance your character. As previously mentioned, criticism is an inherent component of achieving success. However, there is no need to fear it, as it is an opportunity for personal growth and resilience.

Allow me to elucidate the potential benefits that can be derived from the criticism posed by individuals who harbor negative attitudes towards a particular subject matter:

Harness the negative emotions to infuse strong emotional intensity.

Instead of allowing yourself to feel insignificant and devalued due to harsh criticism, redirect your passion and harness its power to fuel positive emotional change within yourself. Pursue the necessary actions to achieve success, transcend the negativity, and harness that energy to propel yourself forward.

Encourage you to clearly articulate your objective.

Harness the power of discontentment to enhance your clarity and sharpen your focus towards accomplishing your goals. Once you establish your objectives and the rationale behind them, you become impervious to any form of criticism. Harness their energy to propel yourself and move forward towards the accomplishment of your aspirations. Demonstrate increased achievements by harnessing their vitality.

Maintains a sense of humility

In the face of a persistent onslaught of hate and negativity, one will undoubtedly find solace in the attainment of success. However, it is crucial to remain grounded and cognizant of the amplified scrutiny and extensive audience that accompany one's path to achieving success. Employ this as a source of motivation and inspiration, to showcase to those who scorn what heights they could reach if they redirected the effort they invest in criticizing towards personal improvement.

Assists in your comprehension of successfully accomplishing the task

Instead of becoming irritated and engaging in verbal conflict with individuals who hold negative attitudes towards you, this experience can serve as an opportunity to exercise moral superiority and choose the path of righteousness. The presence of critics signifies one's accomplishment and competence, as their existence is contingent upon one's ability to excel and thrive. For what reason would they hold animosity towards you?

A tutorial on cultivating greater acceptance and tolerance

Upon gaining firsthand experience, one shall acquire a profound understanding of its impact and thus refrain from replicating such actions onto others. Moreover, it is essential to highlight instances of hatefulness, as this will cultivate a sense of empathy towards others. Furthermore, through your personal experience of navigating and surmounting such challenges, you possess a unique ability to offer guidance and inspiration to individuals who find themselves confronted with comparable circumstances and are struggling to cope.

Utilize the critique for introspection and assessment.

Occasionally, the critiques hold validity, and even in cases where they do not, it is advisable to allocate some time towards self-evaluation in light of the allegations. Please attend to their words, disregard any irrelevant remarks, and embrace the helpful and constructive feedback. Constructive feedback has the potential to enhance one's personal growth and development.

Utilize these resources to acquire techniques for effectively managing conflicts.

Instances of disdain and unfavorable remarks present a valuable occasion for acquiring skills in conflict resolution. By addressing the trials posed by adversaries, one acquires the aptitude to adeptly manage arduous circumstances and adeptly navigate instances of discord.

Anger management

There is perhaps no superior forum for acquiring skills in managing anger than when confronted with adverse feedback from antagonists. This establishment provides an ideal environment for acquiring the skills necessary to maintain composure and refrain from engaging in the face of disparaging remarks, while also learning to regulate and suppress anger.

Ignoring negativity

A positive mental outlook is necessary for achieving success. If one lacks the resilience to confront the negativity stemming from adversaries, they are essentially deviating from a state of optimistic thinking. Detractors can assist you in handling and disregarding unfavorable circumstances, enabling the maintenance of a constructive mindset conducive to achieving success.

Drive for achievement

As previously mentioned, it is advisable to utilize any negative feedback or criticism as a source of motivation to surpass all expectations in your endeavors. Utilizing the pessimism exhibited by dissenting voices can serve as an unparalleled source of inspiration, fortifying your resolve and unwavering commitment to attaining your aspirations.

In summary, it is essential to bear in mind that the critic's disparagement merely represents their subjective viewpoint. Do not place excessive importance on it, as it should not impede or deter you from the pursuit of your goals. It can be quite effortless to succumb to the desires of those who harbor animosity towards you or unintentionally aid them in their endeavors, should you neglect to remain vigilant and unwavering in your resolve. You are likely to face numerous challenges on the path to achieving success, among them being subjected to disdain and hostility. Regard it as an acknowledgment of your efforts and an indication to continue striving diligently. Embrace the power of adversity, allowing the force of animosity to propel you towards achieving remarkable success instead of impeding your progress.

CHAPTER FOUR
VARIOUS FORMS OF DIETARY RESTRICTION

There exist three distinctive forms of fasting, which encompass various approaches to its observance. These encompass

1) The partial fasts pertain to a specific type of fasting practice wherein one refrains from consuming certain foods as a means of showing reverence to God. Culinary offerings such as fine wine and delectable gourmet dishes. This form of fasting is commonly referred to as partial fasting, as it entails refraining from the consumption of a particular beloved or delectable meal. However, with the intention of seeking divine favor, he/she abstains from consuming that particular food for a designated period, as an expression of utmost reverence towards the Almighty, signifying that nothing holds greater importance than their devotion to Him. This can be observed in the experiences of Daniel, as mentioned in the scripture (Daniel 10:3): "I abstained from consuming palatable food, abstained from partaking in meat or wine, and refrained from applying any sort of fragrant oils on my body." Until the completion of a total of three weeks.

Frequently, it possesses a greater length and is accompanied by a deliberative process, with such decisions being subjective and influenced by an individual's spiritual guidance.

2) Complete fasts refer to a type of fasting where individuals limit their intake exclusively to liquids such as water or juice. It has the potential to be prolonged for an extended duration. Certain individuals are capable of undergoing a fast lasting seven consecutive days without consuming solid food, relying solely on the intake of water or juice to sustain their bodily vitality throughout the fasting duration. The juice provides a greater boost of vitality compared to water, nonetheless, the consumption of solid food is strictly prohibited until the fasting period concludes.

We visited the residence of an individual who was afflicted by repeated episodes of spiritual intrusion, resulting in complete paralysis of both lower limbs and rendering him unable to engage in productive labor. As a result, he remained confined to his humble abode, relying on the assistance of his devoted spouse to tend to his needs. I arrived alongside a group of devout individuals dedicated to prayer, and together we made the decision to embark upon a three-day period of fasting in order to intercede on behalf of the family and invite divine presence into their residence. It was a situation in which individuals were released from the influence of malevolent entities, or spiritual assaults, as Jesus instructed his disciple that certain demons are exceedingly resistant and can only be driven out through disciplined fasting and prayer. This was precisely what we practiced, resulting in a triumph granted by God. As a result, the household was rejuvenated, and both the husband and wife, the latter of whom had not previously attended church, began regularly attending all services. The husband has since made a full recovery and is now mobile without any impediments. This illustrates the potential effects of fasting, and we undertook a comprehensive liquid-only fast to demonstrate this. This particular form of fasting contributes to the nourishment of your inner being, encompassing both spiritual and physical dimensions. It will effectively eliminate any accumulated toxins within your body, revitalizing your entire system and resulting in a rejuvenated appearance, as your skin becomes noticeably more radiant upon completion of the cleanse. We commenced our meal with the consumption of juice, resulting in an invigorating sensation within my physical organism, manifesting as a notable lightness in my body and a remarkable freshness in my complexion. This fasting regimen serves as an effective means to exorcise demons or combat malevolent assaults in one's life.

3) The Absolute or dry fasts pertain to a fasting method where the abstainer refrains from consuming any form of water, juice, or sustenance. The body remains devoid of any sustenance throughout the entire duration of this fasting method. The sacred text made

reference to individuals who adhered to these fasts, namely...

a) The apostle Paul, upon his encounter with Jesus while en route to Damascus with the intention of persecuting the followers of Christ (Acts 9:9)

b) According to the scriptures, both Moses (Deuteronomy 9:9) and Elijah (1 Kings 19:8) partook in this form of fasting for a duration of forty days. It should be noted that such an extended fast is of an exceptional nature and can only be maintained through the divine assistance of the Holy Spirit. It is important to recognize that undertaking such a fast without the guidance of the Holy Spirit can pose risks to one's physical well-being.

A prophet embarked on a forty-day journey to the mountain in order to partake in this form of fasting. Unfortunately, on the concluding day, he became incapacitated and was subsequently discovered by individuals who were aware of his seclusion for prayer and fasting. As they endeavored to transport him to the hospital for resuscitation, he passed away. I do not assert that it is impossible to engage in such an action, however, it is conceivable that it may be in accordance with divine instruction or guidance. Do not be swayed by the actions of others; instead, adhere to your inner intuition, and allow divine providence to illuminate your path. I have undertaken a three-day fruit-only fast, abstaining from solid food. However, on the second day, a divine answer was bestowed upon me, wherein I was graced with a profound revelation. Subsequently, I received a clear message to gather my belongings and return home, connoting that my supplication had already been granted, thus obviating the necessity to persevere with the fast. It is imperative to adhere to one's inner intuition and seek enlightenment through prayer in order to acquire a heightened sense of clarity prior to undertaking the fast. All individuals are required to observe fasting in certain significant circumstances, but one must rely on spiritual guidance to discern the appropriate form of fasting that one can undertake.

Laws Of The Universe

"Here's the problem. The majority of individuals tend to primarily focus their thoughts on things they wish to avoid, thus perplexed by the recurring appearance of such unwanted occurrences."

–John Assaraf

To gain a comprehensive understanding of the mechanics behind the process of manifestation, it is prudent to analyze and delve into the fundamental principles governing the universe, more specifically, the two Universal Laws at play.

The Principle of Attraction in accordance with the legal framework

The Law of Attraction holds utmost significance as the preeminent force within the vast expanse of the cosmic universe. This widely notorious legislation materializes your mental constructs into tangible existence. It serves as the primary impetus for all forms of creation. According to this principle, any energy or actions you release into the world will be reciprocated, often referred to as the law of attraction. This signifies that our thoughts, beliefs, and expectations have the capacity to draw corresponding experiences and circumstances into our existence.

Our lives are shaped by the influential force of our magnetic thoughts. Your current thoughts are instrumental in shaping the trajectory of your future existence. Due to your perpetual state of contemplation, you are constantly engaging in the act of generating.

In the process of creation, our minds serve as the initial breeding ground for all that we conceive. Manifestations in our lives are derived from the compelling nature of our thoughts. The artistic process begins with an initial spark of inspiration, which further evolves into the creation of a masterpiece. The initial step in the construction process involves the development of a architectural blueprint, followed by the actual construction of a residence. Our thoughts are the blueprint to creation.

Positive experiences are drawn to individuals who possess strong, affirmative thinking patterns. Love. Happiness. Abundance. These ecstatic sensations are encounters that we all desire. And guess what? They likewise desire our affiliation! As an illustration, when one possesses a belief in their intellectual and professional capabilities, they are bound to achieve affluence.

Pessimistic thoughts possess the ability to greatly disrupt optimistic mental frameworks. Fear. Insecurity. Anxiety. We have all experienced these feelings of dampening joy at some juncture throughout our lives. However, fixating on these matters can be detrimental to one's well-being and progress. The detrimental thoughts you harbor will reflect the adverse experiences you are striving to evade. For instance, if one consistently fixates on the idea of illness, it is highly probable that their desire will eventually manifest.

Regardless of the challenges we face, it is imperative that we redirect our attention towards the inherent aesthetic value found in life's imperfections. Alternatively, what I describe as the pursuit of life's Wabi-Sabi, distinct from the pungent condiment wasabi, can also be regarded as such. It embodies the Japanese philosophy of embracing the inherent beauty found in imperfection. In doing so, we fortify ourselves against the potential influx of undesirable occurrences into our lives.

Once you attain an understanding of the law of attraction, it possesses the potential to greatly alter the circumstances presented in every aspect of your life. You simply need to alter your thought process. You will come to appreciate the immense potency within you, which allows you to effectively manifest your desires through the power of your thoughts.

When individuals hold the belief that the law of attraction is not effective, it often stems from their tendency to focus their attention on the various adversities and shortcomings that exist within their lives. If one limits their television viewing to the pursuit of negative news, they will indeed discover precisely that. To bring about positive changes in your life, the cultivation of constructive thinking is imperative. This implies purposefully determining the point of concentration.

The Law Of Vibration

The Law of Vibration serves as an essential cornerstone that will enable you to harness the potency of the Law of Attraction. In order to lead a truly fulfilling existence, it is imperative that you acquire the skills to excel in this particular area.

The realm in which we reside is governed by the phenomenon of vibrational frequencies. All entities are perpetually in motion and oscillating at varying frequencies. Nothing rests. Frequencies refer to the rate at which objects oscillate, and each oscillation yields energy.

One can experience heightened levels of energy, as well as diminished levels of energy. As the energy increases, so does the vibration, whereas a decrease in energy leads to a decrease in vibration. Positive energy is merely a manifestation of elevated frequencies. When one's vibrations are elevated, they engender states of euphoria such as serenity, affection, joy, and enthusiasm. Negative energy refers to lower levels of vibrational frequencies. These emotions elicit more intense reactions such as rage, animosity, hopelessness, and apprehension.

Objects are in a state of harmonious coherence when they oscillate at congruent frequencies. One would not anticipate encountering a blend of contemporary chart-topping music, commonly aired on the radio frequency 96.5FM, and a selection of classical musical compositions, often featured on the radio frequency 100FM. Indeed, the Law of Vibration operates on a parallel basis. All phenomena that materialize in existence do so by resonating with an identical energy frequency.

The fundamental premise underlying the Law of Vibration posits that through the modulation of our vibrational frequencies, we possess the ability to magnetize and draw towards us the desired elements and manifestations in our existence. For a manifestation to transpire, it is imperative that our thoughts, emotions, and verbal expressions are congruent with our desired outcome. This phenomenon can be understood as a state of being in consonance with the vibrations around one.

Vibrational Harmony

Feelings are among the most influential frequencies that can be managed by an individual. It is crucial to understand that your emotional state is what ultimately dictates your level of Vibrational Harmony. By exhibiting awareness towards your emotional state, it is possible to discern whether you are devoting your attention to your desires or their respective void. This can be achieved by directing your focus towards your own emotions. When your thoughts and desires achieve a state of consonance in terms of vibration, you experience a sense of wellbeing and optimism. The presence of intense sentiments such as ardor, enthusiasm, and delight signifies that your vibrational frequency aligns with your aspirations. Feelings such as concern, frustration, and self-doubt indicate that one's attention is directed towards the lack of desired outcomes, thereby causing a misalignment with one's objectives.

www.ingramcontent.com/pod-product-compliance
Lightning Source LLC
Chambersburg PA
CBHW050243120526
44590CB00016B/2194